LOWEST PLACES ON THE PLANET

by Karen Soll

CAPSTONE PRESS
a capstone imprint

Pebble Plus is published by Capstone Press,
1710 Roe Crest Drive, North Mankato, Minnesota 56003
www.mycapstone.com

Library of Congress Cataloging-in-Publication Data
Soll, Karen.
  Lowest places on the planet / by Karen Soll.
     pages cm.—(Extreme Earth)
  Includes bibliographical references and index.
  ISBN 978-1-4914-8343-5 (library binding)
  ISBN 978-1-4914-8347-3 (pbk.)
  ISBN 978-1-4914-8351-0 (ebook PDF)
1. Physical geography—Juvenile literature. 2. Altitudes—Juvenile literature. 3. Physical
geography—Study and teaching. I. Title.
  GB58.S66 2016
  551.44—dc23   2015025591

Editorial Credits
Karen Soll, editor; Juliette Peters, designer;
Tracy Cummins, media specialist; Tori Abraham, production specialist

Photo Credits
Alamy: Dmytro Pylypenko, 19; Corbis: Luo Sha/Xinhua Press, 21; Marcelo Kovacic: 13;
Shutterstock: Avik, 3, 11, 22-23, Endless Traveller, 15, Felix Lipov, Cover Bottom Left,
Ivsanmas, Map, Nickolay Vinokurov, Cover Top, 17, Ovidiu Hrubaru, 5, S. Bonaime, Cover
Bottom Right, Vadim Petrakov, Design Element, 1; Thinkstock: Anatoly Ustinenko, 9,
Quinn Rooney, 7

Note to Parents and Teachers

The Extreme Earth set supports the Next Generation Science Standards related
to earth science. This book describes and illustrates climate and geography. The
images support early readers in understanding the text. The repetition of words
and phrases helps early readers learn new words. This book also introduces early
readers to subject-specific vocabulary words, which are defined in the Glossary
section. Early readers may need assistance to read some words and to use the
Table of Contents, Glossary, Read More, Internet Sites, Critical Thinking Using the
Common Core, and Index sections of the book.

Printed and bound in China.
007478LEOS16

TABLE OF CONTENTS

LOW PLACES

Tall hills and high places
are all around. The ground
dips low in other places.
Let's find out about these
low places.

A lake in Australia is very low. Rain can fill it. Then it is the biggest lake in Australia.

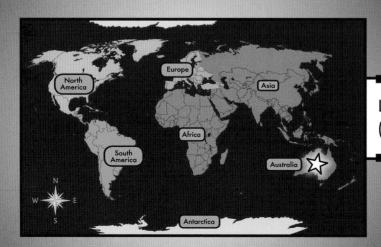

Lake Eyre is 52 feet (16 meters) below sea level.

A body of water is
between Europe and Asia.
This is Europe's lowest point.
It is also the largest lake
in the world.

The Caspian Sea is 92 feet
(28 meters) below sea level.

LOWER PLACES

Death Valley is in California.

It is the lowest place

in North America.

It is hot and dry too.

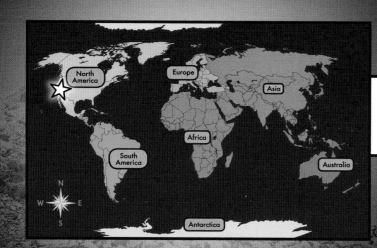

Death Valley is 282 feet
(86 meters) below sea level.

South America has

a lake as its lowest point.

Many rivers drain into it.

Laguna del Carbón is 344 feet
(105 meters) below sea level.

The lowest place in Africa is a lake too! It gets very hot here. The heat turns the water into a gas.

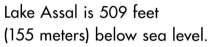

Lake Assal is 509 feet (155 meters) below sea level.

LOWEST PLACES

The lowest point in Asia

is by the Dead Sea.

It is the shore.

The shoreline of the Dead Sea is 1,360 feet (415 meters) below sea level.

A trench in Antarctica is

the lowest point in the world

that water does not cover.

It is cold and icy.

The Bentley Subglacial Trench
in Antarctica is 8,333 feet
(2,540 meters) below sea level.

The Pacific Ocean

has the lowest point.

Only special boats go there.

Would you like to see any

of these low places?

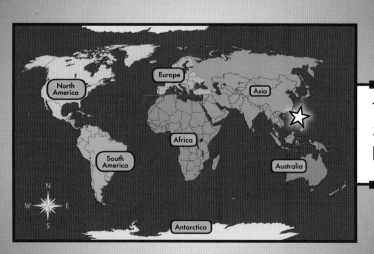

The Mariana Trench is
36,198 feet (11,033 meters)
below sea level.

GLOSSARY

Africa—a continent between the Atlantic and Indian Oceans and south of Europe

Asia—a large continent that contains many countries, including China and India

Australia—a continent in the South Pacific Ocean

Dead Sea—a large salt lake between Israel and Jordan

drain—to flow into something

Europe—a continent west of Asia

North America—a continent in the Western Hemisphere that includes the United States, Canada, Mexico, and Central America

sea level—the average level of the surface of the ocean, used as a starting point from which to measure the height or depth of any place

shore—the place where water meets land

South America—a continent between the Atlantic and Pacific Oceans

READ MORE

Davies, Nicola. *Oceans and Seas*. Discover Science. New York: Kingfisher, 2011.

O'Connell, Bailey. *Earth's Lowest Places*. Earth's Most Extreme Places. New York: Gareth Stevens Publishing, 2015.

Simon, Seymour. *Seymour Simon's Extreme Earth Records*. San Francisco: Chronicle Books, 2012.

INTERNET SITES

FactHound offers a safe, fun way to find Internet sites related to this book. All of the sites on FactHound have been researched by our staff.

Here's all you do:

Visit *www.facthound.com*

Type in this code: 9781491483435

Super-cool stuff!

Check out projects, games and lots more at
www.capstonekids.com

CRITICAL THINKING USING THE COMMON CORE

1. Look at the picture on page 19, and read the text. Why might Antarctica have a low point that water does not cover? (Integration of Knowledge and Ideas)

2. The author says that many rivers drain into a lake in South America. What does it mean for a river to drain into a lake? (Craft and Structure)

3. Heat can turn the water in Africa's lake to a gas. Write about what happens to the water. (Key Ideas and Details)

INDEX

Grade: 1